The Long Experience of Love

Also by Jim Moore

The Freedom of History

Minnesota Writes: Poetry
    (coeditor)

How We Missed Belgium
    (with Deborah Keenan)

What the Bird Sees

The New Body

The
Long
Experience
of Love

∼

Jim Moore

∼

MILKWEED EDITIONS

The Rilke epigraph is from the "Ninth Duino Elegy," translated by Stephen
Mitchell and published in *The Selected Poetry of Rainer Maria Rilke,* edited and
translated by Stephen Mitchell (Random House, 1982). Copyright © 1980,
1981, 1982 by Stephen Mitchell. Used by permission from Random House, Inc.

Published 1995 by Milkweed Editions
Printed in the United States of America
Book design by Will Powers. The text of this book is set in Sabon.
95 96 97 98 99   5 4 3 2 1
First Edition

Milkweed Editions is a not-for-profit publisher. We gratefully acknowledge
support from the Dayton Hudson Foundation for Dayton's and Target Stores;
Ecolab Foundation; General Mills Foundation; Honeywell Foundation; Jerome
Foundation; John S. and James L. Knight Foundation; The McKnight
Foundation; Andrew W. Mellon Foundation; Minnesota State Arts Board
through an appropriation by the Minnesota State Legislature; Musser Fund;
Challenge and Literature Programs of the National Endowment for the Arts;
I. A. O'Shaughnessy Foundation; Piper Family Fund of the Minneapolis
Foundation; Piper Jaffray Companies, Inc.; John and Beverly Rollwagen Fund
of the Minneapolis Foundation; The St. Paul Companies; Star Tribune/Cowles
Media Foundation; Surdna Foundation; James R. Thorpe Foundation; Unity
Avenue Foundation; Lila Wallace-Reader's Digest Literary Publishers Marketing
Development Program, funded through a grant to the Council of Literary
Magazines and Presses; and generous individuals.

Library of Congress Cataloging-in-Publication Data

Moore, James. 1943 –
    The long experience of love / Jim Moore. — 1st ed.
        p.   cm.
    ISBN 1–57131–401–6 (acid-free paper) : $12.95
    1. Love poetry, American.   I. Title.
PS3563.O618L66   1995
811'.54—dc20
                                                                94-32531
                                                                    CIP

This book is printed on acid-free paper.

For JoAnn, Emmy Lou, Madeline, and Mira

Acknowledgments

Thanks to the following journals, where some of the poems in this book first appeared: *11th Muse, The Antioch Review, The Colorado Review, The Kenyon Review, The Paris Review, Poetry East, The Santa Monica Review.* The sequence "How the Dead Block Our View" was originally commissioned by Artpark in Lewiston, New York.

So many people have helped me with this book: friends, editors, fellow poets, and strangers who came along at the right time. Even though I've so often been its recipient, the generosity of people amazes me. I am more grateful than ever: thank you.

For encouragement and help with the "Boy" sequence I want to especially thank Don Brunnquell, David Goldes, Joseph Goldes, Lewis Hyde, Deborah Keenan, Miriam Levine, Joel Janowitz, Sheryl Mousley, and JoAnn Verburg.

I owe particular thanks to my editor at Milkweed Editions, Emilie Buchwald. Her help was crucial in organizing and shaping this book.

I also want to thank The Loft – an organization devoted to helping writers and nurturing literature – for dreaming up an innovative new program called the Minnesota Writers Career Initiative Program, which has made it possible for me to reach many more people with this book than would otherwise have been possible.

I am happy to have the opportunity to thank the students with whom I've worked in recent years. It's been a pleasure to see how much poetry matters in their lives.

Finally, I want to offer special thanks to JoAnn Verburg, who has helped me with so many of these poems and whose presence in my life reminds me to follow Elizabeth Bishop's advice, which I quote at the beginning of this book's first section: "Whatever there was, or is, of love let it be obeyed."

Contents

3

Author's Note

The group of poems I've called "Tagore: Homages and Variations"
emerged from my reading of his collection *Gitanjali*. Rabindranath
Tagore, who died in 1941, was awarded the Nobel Prize in Literature.
His work and ideas continue to be influential in India, especially in
his native Calcutta. Readers curious to explore Tagore's work can find
Gitanjali as well as other selections of his work in *Collected Poems
and Plays* (Collier, 1993).

The short prose pieces toward the end of this book are part of a larger
work about turning fifty. While not poems, these pieces are closer to
poetry in spirit than to the discursive nature and patient explorations
of the true essay. A group of them, written during a trip to Italy and
exploring the book's twin themes of love and loss in a different form,
seemed like the right way to bring this book to a close.

The Long Experience of Love

The Long Experience of Love
(on being photographed while holding a photograph of my mother)

I can see right through her to the world
beyond the porch: a single bird
of paradise and two scaly palms.
When she could still see well enough
to care about shapes in the world,
gardens were the pleasure she most loved
to work in. She is almost weightless
in my hand and keeps shaking,
though I try to hold her still,
so that others may see
what I see: a guardedness that cannot hide
the unmasked plea for love passed down
from mother to son.
Our lives are small things,
easy to miss. The truth is
they do not belong to us at all,
but must, in the end, be returned
to the sky: to that same mottled distance
so like the speckled blue of the bird shell
I found when I was six
and she was thirty-four.
It was broken, that little suitcase,
and the dried and wasted shine
of a fallen life was stuck to the shell.
How I cried then
because of the litter a death makes
when it falls into our world
for the first time. I raise my mother
to the day's last light
for fear she might slip away
into darkness before I've had enough
of looking at her. My mother pretended
to love that broken shell
as much as I did
because this is what mothers do
when their children cry out to them, undone
for the first time by a world in ruins:
they make it seem natural to love what ends.

1

Whatever there was, or is, of love let it be obeyed . . .
– ELIZABETH BISHOP
(undated fragment of a poem)

The Same Life

The life that pulses under my wrist
as blood is the same life
that sways inside summer weeds.
The life that is mine day and night
also belongs to the world.
It is the same life
that rocks back and forth in the ocean,
the same life that opens the gates
at birth, then closes them at death.

Queen Elizabeth on TV

It was my first look at the world
on a small screen: her coronation
in my aunt's living room. It's amazing
how close I came that day to loving
what I saw without question. A small boy
staring at a queen. Both of us were excited.
Both knew it was crazy how things happen
beyond our power to understand them.
The queen and I, we were enchanted: earth
and all its glories seemed enough. Have pity
on us, we who would have loved to rule
our whole lives without incident. We who
have spent our reigns dissolving empires
into warring nations. It was in black
and white, a tiny screen, but it was godly
how she walked down that long aisle alone,
only her heavy train behind her, only
her failing empire before.
We kings and queens cannot help our accidents
of birth: born to rule, born to lose it all.

The Stages of Desire

1

This morning, as you bent your startled eyes
to the mirror, applying darkness
with the eyeliner, I thought of Bellini,
the way surprised faces stare back like that
again and again from his paintings,
as if he could not get enough of amazement.

One cold and windy day in Venice,
the Academia almost empty, I moved
among his figures. In them, the world
was as if whole again, not perfect, but each face
assuming its appropriate strains as I walked
among the shining, pigmented fragments
of our lives. Along the way
a mother suffers, a son dies, and St. George
looks a soldier who'd rather eat pasta than fight,
large-faced George, kind and sleepy
in his armour.

These are the stages of desire: first,
pure conception, then the layered, uneven gradations
of color thickening into life, and finally a transparent sheen
whose very briefness we have even
found a word for: dawn.

2

Two years ago, as your father was dying,
you sat for a few minutes each day at dawn
before your childhood window, while the tree —
at first you barely noticed it, it was hardly
there – called grief made its way towards you
out of the darkness. First, the conception
of suffering, then the thing itself,
until each leaf shone with it under the burden
of its own veined and unprotected shape.
On the final dawn,

his death entered your life
directly, a wordless message.
As once he had entered
your mother, so that you,
his daughter, might finally arrive,
full term, into this grief.

3

This morning when you framed your eyelids
with those most ephemeral of paints, I looked
into the mirror with you, saw past your fresh shadows
into my own watery, near-sighted eyes,
which have seen the small streams Bellini stroked
into his backgrounds, streams where travelers pause
to slake their thirst in the fast-moving water
of a vanishing world.

To Wish It Goodnight

Though my father complained
of the grammar nurses use
when they help take you
out of this world, the truth is
it was not ain't that made him angry.
It had once been so easy
for my father to simply
get up out of a chair
and leave any room he wanted
to be done with.
I saw his eyes follow me
suspiciously, as if it were betrayal
for someone so healthy, his
only son, to walk freely
in and out of the small white room.
But he tolerated the way
I just had to reach
down under two sheets
and touch his foot, a thing
already buried so far
as he was concerned, useless
thing with toes.

He wanted to go on awhile
being my father. Instead,
at 7:24 a.m., he sat up
for the last time and retrieved
one more breath from his thinning air.
He whispered to those of us
who continued to breathe
without even trying,
"She's finally
coming." Then he lay back
to wait, then died.

That night I dreamt my father
took a nap.
Just as he was waking,

the dream ended,
and I, too, woke.
Together, we both left
for our next worlds,
his newly assigned,
mine the same old sunlight,
morning joggers and blue sky.
How near we were
in that dream: he
on the white couch, I
in the brown chair watching
his lovely, clouded eyes open
onto the world.

What I never expected
is how much nothing
there is afterwards.
In life, he was not nearby.
Now he is
everywhere I dream
and every place I wake.
Or if not him exactly,
then a nothing
so much like him
I cannot seem to wish it
goodnight, when I try to sleep.
In death, how completed
the absent one can become.
How easy to lean forward
in the brown chair
and stroke his thinning hair.
He does not mind at all.
He knows that dreams, too,
are part of life.
And death is simply a sentence
that he has just spoken:
but only the beginning
of what he has to say.

During his last days,
when there were tubes for everything
that left and entered
the body, and the nurses
couldn't help but wish
my father was gone
because then he would have been
happier, during
the last days,
I turned on the Cubs
for my father, so he could see
one last failed run
at the Pennant.
After the final out, I
approached slowly
from the left, speaking
clearly, my grammar perfect.
I offered him a grape,
and in this way, I gave my father
his last food by hand,
something small and purple,
as beautiful
as it was useless.

After My Father's Death

Almost a year later, from a train near Innsbruck,
I saw a woman about his age. For a moment
I glimpsed the half-hidden bench where she sat, her face
turned away from the passing train, all that speed
and purposefulness. Her dog slept nearby, its head
under her hand. She sat very straight, her back
against the slats of the bench as if it were a pew
and she staring at the man who dies so slowly
on his Cross. "Sacred Conversations" is the phrase for paintings
that embody her wordlessness, her calm moment
near a meadow, haloed by snow and ragged peaks.
The people in these Sacred Conversations
stand silently, looking down and away from each other, united
by devotion to what they cannot name or fully understand.

My father and I almost stepped outside
our separate frames and spoke our love. Instead, first one of us died
and then the other took a train that passed near
the woman, her sleeping beast and silent mountain.
Who knows, really, why a father and his son
must sometimes spend whole years together, not even
looking at each other. As if a third presence,
perhaps a dying God, demanded their linked aversions,
a Sacred Conversation instead of something
profane, born of this earth and their own small time together.

The Young Men

My father, naked in the photo, young
again, crouched among rocks and water. It's an island,
a time so long ago he is thin,
buttocks tense with the pleasure
of climbing down towards beach and sea.
Who is this man who so loved sunlight,
bare skin? Somewhere inside
all the fathers
are these young men:
virginal, unburdened of thoughtful,
mysterious sons and stubborn, principled daughters.

I have the photo to prove it:
they are climbing down rocks
towards the sea. They are almost
on the beach. They are naked
and happy, filled with delight
to be crouching on the coastlines of uninhabited islands.

The Portrait

You want me lying down and I, too, love the unbuckling,
the slow lowering, alone, onto the old green couch, eyes now
barely open. The camera stands stiffly on its tripod,
a kind of disciple in need of focusing from
someone like you who fusses over sleepers and serves
the world by preserving loss, one image at a time.

At first I track you as you move above my body.
Stretched out near sleep, I am the helpless universe you need,
someone about to lose himself to dreams, to disappear
beyond any purpose or hope a waking world can solve.
Alert and intense, you hover above me.
Meanwhile, I fall asleep. For me, it's just another nap.

This time I'm gone longer than usual. When I wake
you've moved the gladioli behind my pillowed head.
Arms crossed over my chest, I feel refreshed and calm,
as if, waking at my own funeral, I find that death is simple,
not like life at all. I lie still and wait for you to finish.
It's love that lets me trust you with my sleep, arrange my death.

Death brings out the best in me. These portraits help me see the soul
I might have been, set free from useless fears. I see a man
I forgot I knew, someone subsumed by stillness without
regret. I wake to see myself as you do, a calm one
at rest, a little dazed, still posing from his sleep, as if
first comes the letting go of life; and only then, the wakefulness.

The One Left Behind
Constable at the Tate

1

You can't stand the puppies, the blurred red blobs
of the shepherds with their crooks, or the little girls
in modest blues. It is possible to simply detest Constable.
But even you will admit his sky
into your life, how relentlessly he moves it,
that ghostmine of lost silver,
passing it from painting to painting.
Here's one with some thick fog in it
where the shepherd is barely visible,
just a sliver of a crook, and the dog
a dog, not a symbol of that tamed landscape,
man's best friend.
And in this one, *Sketch for Hadleigh Castle*,
finished in twenty-eight when his wife died,
clouds open and close, as a body will,
under the needy hands of another.

2

I keep staring at the postcard
next to the bed where you sleep.
I am careful to make no noise.
Soon you will wake refreshed and angry at the sentimental,
in love with this actual London sky,
full of unfallen rain. The rain waits for us
as it did for Constable, to find a path through it,
so that the distance in our souls might move closer,
our cloudy souls which fall towards us in rain,
as grief. All this,
the one who was left behind helped us see,
he who bordered his desolation with a fierce silver line
and called it the sea, that horizon beyond which even he could not go.

How the Dead Block Our View

(Three poems from a collaboration with photographer JoAnn Verburg)

Indian Mound in Winter and Summer

In Memoriam: Jane Hicks Verburg and James Wallace Moore

When snow falls, it transforms all it touches,
shifts what we thought was the shape of the world
into something simpler. Here's where the dead
huddled together for warmth under their hill.
Sometimes the dead seem to block our view
as do these photos; as leaves now block the mound,
or the mound itself, which once housed
another people's dead. It is difficult
to see to the other side of what grieves us.

I want the patience of a lens,
to look a long time at the screen
these photos make of winter, and the new season
that grows all around them. I want the love
that standing still can give us when we learn
to look carefully at how the past
lies mounded within the present. I want
the love that comes from seeing what it is
we can neither go beyond nor turn away from.

Haiku / Touch

Do not feel lonely.
The disappearing world longs
for you to touch it.

Hold Up Winter

Hold up the tree. Hold up the world
as well as you can in heavy wind. Find a friend
to help you. Hold up the skeleton, a photo of bones in black and white.
Hold up the core of the world with bare hands.
Hold up the map, the route from tip to branch,
trunk to root. Hold up for everyone, the core
beneath the leaves, the totem that is hidden
under abundance. Hold up winter, that shivering truth,
the season that refuses to bloom. Hold up
the memory of another time. Try to obscure
the present, to distract it from its wish
to rule the world. Hold up the blueprint,
the soul of the tree. Don't stand too close
to the world as it seems. Back up, then look up
into the bareness of things before they learn
to hide behind their green. Hold up the image
of what remains, even at those final times
when all seems shorn of life. Remember
to wish only for what you need. Hold up
the simplest tree of all; a totem woven from light
and the barest of branches. Hold up –
here in the windy, green-leafed present – the memory
of what once was simple and bare, of what
did not require us to hold it still as it grew
silently, and with purposes of its own, on the empty hill.

Fate

Long after they were asleep,
I'd put my nose to the floor
and crawl into the room
where each night my parents laid out
their huge bodies, one to a bed,
and then said nothing for six, eight,
ten hours. It seemed so perfect, two
that way, why not make it three?
I rested then, like God
on the seventh day. As if it was I
who had created them.

Just as now, on the train to Rome,
so then, too, summer was best.
During the day, I couldn't wait
to return to that room and pick
a bed in the damp cool
of the newly-invented air conditioning.
He was at work, she was somewhere else,
I was alone with the dog, the coolness, the mystery
of the Hardy Boys and *The Case of the Missing Green Bowl.*
On top of the neatly made bed that belonged to those
who made me, I knew the mystery that was most purely mine:
that those who caused me seemed underneath me,
holding me up, but not interrupting a thing, letting me
drift in my own absorbed way
towards the novel's tidy conclusion.

And now, too, it comes up to me
from underneath, this momentary sense that all of it –
the landscape steeped in sun and shadow, the boy
next to me with his backpack, the dream I woke from
in which I'd said to Deborah, "The strange man
in the mirror, is this really me?" –
is simply one more page to turn

on a hot summer's day. All along,
it was the mystery that brought me such pleasure,
the actual turning of pages, the excited fear
and curious sense of relief that come
when it's clear beyond a doubt
that something is missing from the world.

Try thinking of death this way,

as the landscape within which the finished body
is one more incidental: as rocks are,
and moonlight, as dark pines and the white
filaments of a few clouds in the far distance.

I Knew You Were There

We who are bound to time
have no time to lose. Therefore,
we are always late, and in this
we take a strange comfort.

And so, my life has passed,
giving what time I have to those
who seem to need it. Meanwhile, I forget
to give anything to you, you
who ask for nothing.

Even when my father died,
you were there, late that night
as my mother and I sat on her small porch
listening to the ones who find their voices after dark,
crickets and nighthawks. I knew you were there
because I did not think to ask, "Mother,
what time is it now, where has he gone?"

I see now by the light death casts
and the barrier of time breaks up inside me.
What a treasure it is, this new carelessness I feel—
things that I longed for, things that I got—
finally, I can let them go. Who is there to say
that we have done too much or too little?
I will no longer need my coyness
or the sweet way I have of hiding in corners.
My work now is to crown death with life.

Boy

*(A sequence of poems written to
a child who was never born)*

TAGORE: HOMAGES AND VARIATIONS

The Gift
for Lewis Hyde

*I make of my sorrow
a small gift for you. It is so little
to offer, but if I were a beautiful dead one –
a star in your black sky – I would give you,
gladly, my one shining death. Wealth and fame
are tokens you decided to give
or withhold. But this sorrow
that I offer is absolute
and has no strings attached.
Tears are a grace unquestioned,
an offering I have never found you to refuse.*

1 Boy

You would have found my chest
without even trying, and under
each of your arms
I would have found you. Boy,
you would have had the perfect black hair
of your mother, but those blue eyes
would have been mine,
mine, mine.

The doctor picks you up afterwards, after
the long journey, and it makes you cry
to arrive here, in this world.
Because you have already worked harder
than you will ever have to work again,
you are wrapped in a clean white cloth
and laid in your mother's arms.

On your first night,
I would have held you
up to the window,
as if you could see the moon: you
who only hours before would have finished your work
as a tide. *Moonlight,*
I would have whispered in your ear,
then carried you back to your crib
where you would have fallen asleep
again, even before I knew
I was saying good-bye.

2   Darkness

I never wished you anything
but a father
when the darkness comes,
that and hide
and seek at dusk:
there is no
happiness like holding out
alone in darkness, hot
and sweaty, waiting
to be found, your
whole life ahead of you.

Darkness
understands best by feel,
the way a glove does,
taking the fingers one
by one, emptying them
of touch.
Darkness
is where light lets you go
when you need to be
alone, a place
beyond explanation, even
to a son. But you
already know how I love
what can't be explained:
you.

3   The Sea

If you had been born
in the usual way, into the nearness
of a body, the scent of an actual
specified flesh, if you could
walk beside me in the sand,
you would see for yourself
the heaving spirit,
the pooling flesh
of the sea,
and I would not need to say
the obvious then, how it
roots and teems in
our blood, mirrors our souls
in the ripped lair
of its invisible depths.

Sometimes I can't stand
how ceaseless you are,
how ready
to come back to me again
and again, wave after wave
of you almost
existing. Like the sea,
you are always ready
to begin again, and like the sea
you never give up. You are
that shoreless thing
inside me, ripping
and soothing. Just as you
would have had a thumbprint
all your own, so the sea
is a signature. Don't
even think of counterfeiting it,
you'll never get it right.
Let the sea sign its name
to our lives, since everything
about it is teaching me
how to miss you.

4   Morning Then

I tell you what I've told no one
because you don't exist
and because you are so deep
inside me: he worked
my nipple with his fingers
and everywhere he could harden me,
I did. Can you believe it,
fifteen already, and I didn't know yet
how good I could feel
just because someone knew
to pour cheap champagne
into me and then where to put
his hand?

Once surprised like that,
you never forget your body
owns you. You are its toy,
and it spins you
out of control. You never
forget his name, the one
who rubbed your face
in pleasure, who betrayed you
into need. Then,
boy, it is dawn
and my blue pajamas
are back on again, the name tag
right where my mother sewed it,
so as to avoid any confusion
about what goes next to my skin.

On the morning after,
I open the curtains,
then the French doors and stand naked
from the waist up in first light.
He keeps sleeping
behind me on the bed, his
ankles so white, like roots

upended and exposed
to the sun.
Dawn is just so perfect
when you're fifteen
and on the Riviera, the sea close enough
you can smell it, along with
the dried cum from where
he took you.

The very idea of morning
then is beautiful to me. My life
is in ruins, but I don't
see it yet, how yesterday
I had been a boy and now
I am one no more. He began
by teaching me Shakespeare,
how to trust what is foreign
to the tongue. Only afterwards did he take
my penis for his own. "I love you,"
he said and sent me out into the world.

After he is finished with me, his hands
nowhere in sight, I drink white coffee
from a white bowl, then ride
the bus, my new secret life
curled up between my legs.
When I leave the bus, there are Matisses
in the white house on the hill
near the place where a boy
in a black mask and cape keeps
riding his bike in a narrow circle, chanting
Zorro est arrivée. Inside, there are
the odalisques, so cheap looking,
so dark eyed and available, I
want them, they could be me
all spread out like that, waiting
to be used.

5   If You Will Let Me

When you begin
to touch yourself
in secret,
I will say to you
what no one said to me
back then:
I love you.
Back then,
I would let nobody
touch me but myself, and then
only under heavy sheets
of running water, when all alone
I'd coax my erection
out of hiding and no one
was there to make me regret
the small cry
I gave at the end.
When you think no one else
can stand to touch you
but yourself, if you will
let me, I'll rub
your back from the down
of your small shoulders, all
along the knotted spine, that
abacus where shame
strings itself along
the body. About kneading
the small, unviolated back
of my son, no one has a thing
to teach me.

6   From a Distance

Maybe what you want for me
is to move away from you.
Alright then, I can do that,
I can love a thing that actually
exists. In the spirit of what might have become
you, I lift my eyes to the body
of the city. I watch how
it clothes itself in darkness
as dusk turns into full night
and I remember my mother
bending towards me in black
velvet, red lipstick, perfume stuck
to her flesh. How excited I was for her
that she was leaving,
for one whole night,
the son who could not give her
happiness. I look
into the city's darkness
with the same love, expecting
nothing, as I once looked
into my mother's darkness, the same
look you must give to me, you
who can expect nothing from me,
as I bend towards you, nothing except
the perfume of existence,
which cannot help but cling
to everything I do.

You Know How It Is

You know how it is.
On the day summer came looking for me
in order to complete itself inside my heart,
I forgot to look up. There was this vague sweetness
and I felt such longing . . .

2

And whoever walks a furlough without sympathy walks to his own
funeral, dressed in his shroud . . .
–WALT WHITMAN, *Leaves of Grass*

Into the World

Mother, sometimes I am afraid to move.
Let me go now
into the world. Don't try to hide me
behind my gifts. They are meant
to be given away. Mother,
I am human like everyone else,
common as breath, branded with desire, saved by touch.

Think of the World as a Week Alone

As if someone said, *go*, then you went,
and this was what you were given: a night
at St. Martin's-in-the-Fields, a long evening
with the next-to-last of Beethoven's quartets.
You tried to listen as if listening
were all. But in that interval between movements,
where Beethoven intended only silence
to accompany the intense and fussy preparations
for the unfinished music that lay ahead,
shouts and screams entered from across the street
in front of the South African embassy, whitely
chaste like an untouched wedding cake.

Think of the world as a week alone in a strange city.
But think of it especially as this one night
when after the concert, nearby at Trafalgar Square,
two women stood together, oblivious
of you, and said their good-byes.
The one getting on the bus was in tears.
The other, older, more sure of herself and stronger,
said, *pray for me*. Then, in case
it wasn't absolutely clear, said again, demanding it
calmly, *pray for me*. The other had no choice
in the matter. Then,
just as you were sure it was over,
she leaned out of the window to her friend, *I
love you*, she said, and it was so unbearably true
the three of you each stood a moment, stunned, not thinking
of what had to happen next: that the bus must take her away.
The demonstration was fading, hundreds of black balloons
had been released in the name of a freedom
that exists somewhere: if not in this world,
then surely in one someplace nearby.

When the 24 arrived, you sat upstairs,
a moon on your left as you moved up Charing Cross
and took the long way back, Camden Town,
Highgate, and all the rest. By the end of the route,
you were famished. At the Curry Paradise
they put you by the window, but you'd had enough
of the world for one day. It was time for a postcard
to someone familiar, someone from your other country.
Think of the world as a week alone, you began to write.
On the reverse was Keats' House.
You could have walked there after dinner
if you'd wished, could even have stood alone
in the darkness under his favorite tree, the one
he wrote of more than once. But you didn't
want to push your luck too far.
Think of how you just happened to appear
this week and no other, at the exact moment two friends
said their good-byes overheard by you
who had nothing more important to do, not then, not ever,
than to stand like that in the middle of such parting.

Think of the world as a strange city,
only partly yours. Think of it as a silence that should have
let you rest between movements, but didn't. Think
of it as black balloons released into a blacker sky,
as a moment under a famous tree
that almost happened, or as the plush paradise
of a dark booth: spiced and unfamiliar food. You were so hungry,
and this is the meal you wanted, the one you needed to eat.

With Timmy, In and Out of Prison

1

From the very first, Timmy and I were a pair, each of us
with our curly hair and bushy sideburns
cropped to regulation length, each of us
with our hunger for words with more syllables
than we would ever need. College
and degrees, textbooks and research papers, were as exotic
to Timmy as his Kansas City – full of good luck
and bad, fast and dirty, hot and black –
was to me.

Timmy was proud and quiet, stubborn
and easy to offend.
I never learned what he had done
to end up in prison. There's an etiquette
about such things: you don't ask
and are rarely told. Men in prison seldom speak
of where they've been or where they are;
the future is the only place to be.
But I kept waiting for him to tell me,
to sit me down one night after yet another
macaroni and cheese dinner and say,
"It was like this, see. One night
I got a little too high and . . ."
But that conversation never happened.
Nor the one about our pasts,
or the secret hurts
we had carefully nurtured
for years. Instead, we talked about
the easy things: Marxism, modernism, ecology,
theories that would solve the world
of our fears. At the time, it seemed enough.

2

We looked through magazines together,
especially the ones with pictures
of a countryside in full seasonal bloom.

We paused long over Vermont trees in fall,
over cold mountain streams slowly warming
in spring sunlight, or winter birch trees
drifting in several feet of cresting snow.
We looked at them the way a traveller
looks out the window of a train
passing through beautiful countryside,
mesmerized by what our hands could not touch.

Timmy and I decided to write essays.
His were always on Africa, ancient tribes
that meant little to me. How carefully
he bent over the white page, pencil
in hand, his eyes so close to the paper
he seemed to be examining it
for defects. Together we made a language
of our love for ideas. We wrote
with the same longing with which we watched
the seasons change in the pages
of those glossy magazines we loved.
No one has ever
demanded more from theory than Timmy.
Some people have a taste for questions,
for living in ambiguity; but Timmy needed answers,
explanations of the world that would hold.
He'd lived with enough unanswered
and unanswerable questions
to last a lifetime.

3
My white friends said we'd never make it.
His black friends said the same.
But fate had given us
a shared captivity, this strange mirror
in front of which we could stand
and admire our own sense of possibility.
After all, this *was* 1970

and we believed in change as if it were a god
that could do us no harm.

One evening we thumbed through the magnificence
of Victoria Falls, turning
the pages of an old *National Geographic*,
Timmy shaking his head
at the immaculate blacks in crisp whites
staring down at all that falling water
from behind the guardrail where they had transported
the equally awestruck, equally crisp-looking whites in their care.
"Man, you and I shouldn't be looking
at all these happy niggers carrying luggage
for white dudes. They're setting a bad example
for you. Don't you think I'm going to take you
and your suitcase to any waterfalls
when we get clear of here, my man."
He laughed but there was a tension
lurking behind the easy joke
that marked a boundary
we had so far avoided crossing.
Then we both yawned and called it a night,
happy for each other's company,
though nothing of significance had happened
unless you could say getting through one more day
in that place was in and of itself a sort of triumph.

4

Maybe it would have gone on like this indefinitely,
the pleasant monotony of friendship
in a place with so few pleasures.
But one afternoon I forgot for a moment
that happiness was dangerous in prison:
it made you forget where you were.
I decided to visit Timmy in the laundry room,
where men shouted over the hiss and smoke
of huge silver machines that tore at the dirt

in the wrinkled pants and shapeless,
unloved shirts. Timmy and I could be
friendly apparitions together there
in the midst of all that steam, forgetting
for whole moments at a time the prison
that surrounded us on all sides.
When I came in that day, Timmy
was bent over a laundry cart,
sorting clothes. Since I didn't know
how to touch a male friend whom I loved –
the easy movement to arm or shoulder,
or that quick brushing across hair – I snuck up instead
and gave him a light kick on the butt
as if we were both kids in college,
male freshmen in search of their adult lives,
yet willing to take time off for adolescence
with friendly pokes in the ribs and mock-angry grabs.

Timmy whirled when I touched him,
keeping low, his stomach protected to avoid
the knife he assumed his assailant
was about to use. Then he rose up
into my stunned face, his left hand
already shaped into a fist, his right
at my throat and open, the way a claw is open
when it is about to slash.
I understood instantly
that my life was at his mercy.
He saw that it was me
and pulled back. But slowly,
as a partner might pull back
after a dance he is reluctant
to see end. "Don't never,
ever, come up behind me like that again.
You just can't *do* that."

A few seconds later, he apologized.
But in that instant when he had been
at my throat, we both saw the distance
crackling between us, palpable and spiked,
a current that we went to elaborate lengths
not to touch from that day forward.
We let up after that on the home-brewed beer
we used to share together in bitter little sips,
let up on the way we checked in daily.
I was sad and angry, but mostly confused.
I had no idea what to do.

   5
I gave him my address
just before I got out. We imagined
our first reunion
in his Kansas City, or maybe
at a pig roast in my green Iowa.
Even then, I think I knew
we never had a chance. Within three days,
Here Comes the Sun was all I could hear
as I danced in the living room
of an Iowa farm house. My eyes
were closed, my entire life
ahead of me, and now
I could assume the next moment
in a way that Timmy never had
and never would, in
or out of prison. I was free
to turn my back on anything
I wanted. I was home in my America.

Here Comes the Sun
was a whole other life
and I tried to live it as long
as I could. The failure
of that music is another story,

but in the meantime I was twenty-seven,
three days out of prison and already
Timmy was as far away from me
as those scenes in the glossy photographs
when we'd sat on a bunk and imagined
Summer, Spring, Winter, Fall,
beautiful weathers unfolding page by page
for us in an America
even I knew did not really exist. Already,
our life together no longer seemed real.
I didn't know it yet, but the doors
of a different prison had just swung shut.

And that should have been the end of it.
Except that a year later, he called.
He was finally out, too.
His voice was low and cool, far away.
He wanted a place to stay for a few days,
and could he come visit? He needed
to "get away" he said and laughed.
I heard a little of the old Timmy in that giggle,
pleased with himself to have found
just the right words. I was afraid, but said, yes, sure,
of course, man. Hey, it'll be great.
He said he'd call when he had the flight number and day,
but he never did, and I never heard from him again.
I was relieved. Then ashamed
of that relief.
How quickly he became for me
one of those beautiful small towns
profiled in the glossy magazines we'd loved
in spite of ourselves, a stylized happiness
so full of hope it seems exotic now, unreal, barely
of this world at all.

6:30 a.m. / The Sounds of Traffic

The man who was my friend
is my friend no more. When the light
finally comes, I, too, will find my place; I, too,
will sit behind a wheel and steer.
When we are gone from this earth,
who will care that my friend and I fought?
Soon enough, I will fasten my seat belt and turn
on the news. As usual the world will be a sad
and dangerous place. To whom, then, will I speak
of this sadness, of the danger that is everywhere?
To whom, if not to my friend?

Here, There

Here, it's a beach day, or will be soon. Fog will lift,
people quickly appear from everywhere at once,
some with books, some simply with their bodies open to the sun.

There, it has snowed all over the revolution. "So far
you have come," the librarian said to the man
from network news. She walked him through the ruin of her books.

It is good to get away from too much useless work,
from snow. Bare flesh is the first step towards letting go. Small girls
kneel in the sand, smoothing wet pebbles with their open palms.

"I'm glad to be alive because so many friends are dead
and I must work for them and hope." She held a charred book
above the snow. The camera zoomed in on blackened pages.

Let the men in suits rule the world. Leave us alone. Let us
lie next to each other, Australian pines behind our backs,
such a short life ahead. So few days in which to understand.

She let the pages fall onto the white ground and spoke
of the unreadable ruined world, her home, Romania.
She clutched what was left in her gloved hand and looked straight at us.

We lug a stack of books with us to the beach. It's best
to come prepared, though in the end we usually sit and stare
at the waves. As if the world out there has news for us.

She said, "This book's dead, but it's alive." Some of the pages
still burned around the edges, a persistent smoldering glow.
Her work: to catalogue the loss, to make her life our news.

No, we never know what we might want at the beach, dozing
as the new year begins, seduced into calm by the sound
of waves. Never know which page will come to hold our news.

"Before, in those other conditions, books were a form
of breathing. We do not have a theory," she said,
"we do not know in which world we live."

In Romania

She carries the cross, he carries the coffin.
When the dead one is so small, such weights
are possible. The unpaved street is gray,
textured with rain. It's a one-lane village
and the two of them are perfectly balanced:
grave marker and coffin – baby inside –
weigh the same. Tonight the moon is full
and beauty will make its glittering pitch.
The ones who were parents will be at home,
maybe sitting silently with friends. Someone
might nod towards the window and say,
"the moon." The woman who was a mother
could look up a moment from her grief
and track the unearthly light. Many people
will respond if called like that. For the most part,
we are a willing race. And if a friend,
brave enough to sit through such a time,
chooses to say quietly and without joy,
"the moon," the least one can do is look up
and watch as beauty treads its usual path.

January 1, The Beach

The daughter wears a long T-shirt.
She's four at most, in search
of the shallowest wetness she can find.
She already knows "no,"
and "careful now." She already
believes the warning about a bad world, a wave
on top of a shark on top of an over-
your-head mindless tangle of salt water
and sea wind and going down forever.
The whole point of the game is to hold
a plastic bucket as a prop and skip
to the edge of the world as she knows it.

Her older brother is short haired, pale, intense: he's just
too busy to waste time on her. His work:
to order the most excellent and perfect shells
to come towards him out of the surf.
She would scoop them up
in indiscriminate fistfuls. His passion
is for the perfect glistening shape,
wet and gasping for air like a face
under tears. One at a time, as if shelving
expensive delicacies, he places them in his pail.

Mother's butt is on the blanket,
her toes dug in under shells and sand.
Her wandering glance refuses
all loyalty: she looks from magazine
to horizon, spends more time
eyeing her nails carefully
than watching her children.
The delicious sag of her body
says it all: she's on this beach
for the laziness. Let him
do it this time, the first
child watch of the day, the year.

And he does do it.
The husband and father stands behind
his fishing pole, not watching
the line for fish at all, instead
tracking the T-shirt-enveloped
four-year-old and the serious boy
of ten. The pole is his prop
and he holds it towards the water
like an offering.
He keeps jerking his head
back and forth, as if trying
to look in all directions at once.
It's how his whole body keeps stumbling
against the surrounding air
that tells me this trembling
is unending. It goes
where he goes. It is his only home.

The fishing pole shakes
in his hand, and his hand shakes
against the bulky, unstable shore
of his body. At night, he must stare
at the place where darkness pools
on the bedroom ceiling. Does his wife
just lie beside him, her stillness
a kind of reproach, his right hand
on her left, working the space
between his body and hers?
Or does it matter
as long as their skins shine together
in the velvet clasp of flesh against flesh?

When the fish strikes, not one of us
is ready. The woman jumps to her feet,
the girl shrieks as she runs
towards her father, the boy
lets his pail fall and all of us

watch the man at the slippery task
of bringing it in. It's a beauty, too:
silver, huge, flailing away
at the universe of air and light.
In the moment of surprise,
as the fish leaps, the man's neck
forgets to shake or jump. He grows
as still as a concert hall
in the long moment after the last note falls
into silence and everything is solved,
momentarily, before the applause.

It is time now
for me to go home. The show is over.
The family on the beach stays behind.
They have their fish
and their day at the shore before them.
Later, I will go to the grocery store
where the young woman works
whose baby died. She decided to stay
in this small town by the sea.
"That way I'll always know the names
of the streets where he would have walked,"
she said once when I was leaving
with my milk and bread. "Thank you
for listening," she said as I left.
As if her grief and her love were things
she'd owed me, a kind of debt.

Today's Meditation

I like it right here,

new light and old darkness under the weightless sky
and the business of shadowy chimneys unburdening into red.
It is time for the first of the birds to be called down
from the invisible. No reticence

like the reticence of a sky newly retrieved from darkness.
I'll never have to be God or anything like the wind
that goes everywhere, knows everything. Our hands met

in darkness last night as we watched TV, the Sister
somewhere in Lebanon and the spastic young man
in his diaper, how their eyes met, as her left palm

opened against the terrible ribs under his stomach
and slowly stroked him into peace. He leaned back on the pillow.
He slept then. And that, too, is a function of love, how it

lets us sleep, even in the midst of such pain.

The Necessary Strength

Just a little strength is best,
so that I may bend lightly
under the weight
of my joys and sorrows. Only enough
not to ignore the woman
sleeping in the street,
the man who makes a morning
of going through the neighbor's refuse.
Just a little strength, enough
to resist a greater strength gone bad.

3

As for me, one evening that nobody noticed, which I myself could
not distinguish from my other evenings, I began quite imperceptibly
to love. Not a woman, or my mother, or brother, or sister –
indeed, at the time I was only a few years old. I began to love
generally somehow, in the form of having a readiness for it, but
with determination, like a ship setting out for the open sea whence
there is no return. And thereafter, into my love, onto my ship,
embarked and disembarked all the fellow travelers of my fate,
sharing with me for a while the same wash of the waves, ebb of the
tide, sun and winds.
– MILORAD PAVIĊ
(translated by Christina Pribicevic-Zoric)
from *The Inner Side of The Winds,*
or The Novel of Hero and Leander

In the Meantime

From early morning to late at night,
I sit in this little park
where shadows and light play with each other,
hoping that one day the time will come
when I can truly see.
But in the meantime,
I sit here
singing under my breath.
In the meantime, the air is heavy
with the promise of rain,
and the sweetness that follows rain.

Preparing for Fifty

For Mary Rockcastle on the occasion of her 40th

It came to me that I needed a valley.
It came to me that I was done with the salmon
as my totem, how it scrapes its way upwards over rocks,
how the body quivers and strains, as if waiting
to be touched for the first time. All that is fine
for thirty, even forty, but for two years now I've believed
in fifty, someplace where who I am counts for more
than who I might become. Last week at long last,
I found a valley where I could be the small thing
for once. I could lie down in the hot springs and just be
covered. I swayed there in the water and waited
for the calm that becomes a body at fifty.
It came to me how to be at home on my back,
my genitals floating above me, an obscure species
of water lily drifting back and forth,
hardly attached to the long and clumsy root
of the body. Soothed and silenced by water, it was here
that my life has brought me, wrinkled as the day I was born.
This time around I was calmer, more sure
of how water and earth work together to offer me up
to the valley. As if I were a human sacrifice,
given up in the name of love, baptized in water, flesh
and blood in the valley of stone until the last breath.

The Task at Hand
(downstairs neighbor)

My friend who is afraid peeled an apple
under kitchen light. I barely paused
on the back stairs, going up with laundry,
and saw a woman overwhelmed by the lacks
that have begun to collect themselves:
the deaths of friends, an older sister,
the grandchild born too soon.
Then there are the sudden cancers
on her skin, one like a blind eye,
red and empty of all purpose, blistering her forehead:
as if she were a worshipper who had tried to scrub it away,
no longer believing in sight by mystery.

I woke this morning and thought of you, my friend,
how the night before you were standing by your sink,
attentive only to the task at hand
as you worked the apple to its opened flesh.
If only we could see ourselves
as the momentary souls we are,
almost finished before we have truly begun. Surely
we would have such mercy on ourselves
that even our griefs and fears
would become part of the work that feeds our souls,
that devoted attention to the task at hand
wherever it may lead us, that *is* our souls.

In the Café: The Grown Daughter

Suddenly the daughter puts her left hand to the forehead
of her mother. As if to mark the furrow with the cross
that only love can bear. As if she is the priest
and her mother the penitent. She tries on
the mother's sunglasses. But they are too large
and there is so much darkness behind them.
Then the mother begins to speak. The daughter sighs deeply,
inhales the bitter smoke of a cigarette,
as the story unfolds for more than an hour.
Finally the daughter pushes away
from the table, pushes away slowly
as if it is the smooth body
of a lover to whom she says at last,
no, enough. She leaves. The mother looks around
at all the tables where no one sits whom she loves.
She looks longest at the girl who reads alone
at the counter, absorbed in *The Diary*
of Anne Frank. For a moment it seems as if the mother
might interrupt the girl. But no: what, after all,
can be said to a child lost in the story
of another's life? Streetlights come on. The mother
puts her sunglasses away. Now it is time to smile good-bye
to the man behind the counter. To look at the girl in love
with the girl in her book. Nobody interrupts anybody: the story goes on.

Freshman Papers

Like orange candywrappers, writes
the daughter now, describing the time
years ago when the goldfish
were thrown into the street
after her mother died.
Like litter, but still
trying to swim. And then,
there's the young man
whose father flew over Hiroshima,
just afterwards. My student wanders
around in prose until
he discovers why his father never speaks
of what he feels: *Maybe he saw*
too much death even before
I was born. The son tries to forgive
the father in paragraph eight.
Title: *My Father the Stranger.*

If I only had
one mistake to take with me, red pen
in hand, into the grave, I'd choose
surprise: those misspelled words that drop
the undeserving reader
without warning into *hys-*
terical, rather than *his-*
torical, or *it's a doggy*
dog world. And truly, it's a dog
eat dog world. Take the daughter
who just last year
remembered the neighbor's zipper
when she was six, then seven, then eight,
how it scratched her cheek, how carefully
he dried her face.

Daily,
I spoil their terrors
by pleading in the margins

for more or less.
I grade what I can and leave
the rest to them to revise
as they must, these sons
and daughters with their lost subjects
and ruinous verbs, their bent heads
just inches above the paper
when they write in class,
free hand cupped around the words they form
so that no one will see before
they do, how it is their lives
turned out, now that I have asked.

Near Herons

1

With the sun a full inch above the horizon, comes
the wind. The old man, becalmed in a white shirt, stands
with hands in pockets before the world's freshening,
the water in the bay beginning to shrug and shiver under the spur
of the raw, still unsettled light. Think of them, old men
all over the world sliding on their shoes in the dark,
by feel alone. Old men who do not wake their wives,
but step quietly out on the grass or sand
and stand in a place where they can see the sun
rejoin the world once again.

2

It is my pleasure to think of the men: my need
to see them facing open water near herons,
ordering nothing to happen
in these, the last days of their lives.
Near herons who know how to leave earth for miles
at a time. Creatures who, when stirred, open their wings
without a sound and lift themselves into another world.

In Rome, I Ran the Tiber

It was dawn in a great city
and I was a grown-up in short shorts,
out of place and a little frightened.
Not a soul in sight. The Tiber
churned wide and deep beneath me,
as I crossed a bridge and took a hill.
A baby cried.
I looked in all directions for an infant
left by the road at dawn in Rome,
until I heard another, then a third.
The cries were floating down from above.
Angels? It was Rome, after all,
and there was nothing frantic in the cries.
These were babies who knew that soon enough
what they wanted would come.
But when I looked up, I saw a dilapidated,
sprawling hospital, the maternity wing.
And then, before I knew it, all Rome
was below me, hundreds of silver domes
slipped inside the watery smoke
of day's first wavering light.

I might have stopped right there,
but then I would have missed
the merry-go-round and the two women
in white smocks – they could have been nurses
on break from the hospital – who ran it.
The music was on and the horses,
riderless, were rising and dipping.
The women watched me expectantly,
as if, perhaps, I had run all this way
to be the first, so that I might have
any horse I wanted
and ride in splendor
in a small circle high above Rome.

Somehow I missed my turn
for the hotel and ended up, alone
and panting, at the Forum. All
I'd ever hoped for from running
every day, even when I don't
want to, is the feeling of having achieved
a small, expected virtue. To enter
the Forum that way, alone, surrounded
by the fragments of an ancient power, meant
that once again life was stranger
than I wanted it to be,
less expected, less achieved.

When the cry of a baby
comes floating down from above,
it is only demanding what is all of ours
by right of birth: to be brought
from afar the milk we need,
and then to be held
until we sleep so that we may dream
of our overwhelmed lives, lives
that were never meant to be jogged,
only suckled, then held, then allowed
to grow up until they become
just too much. It's so good
to take a shower afterwards,
after trying to pace myself
so that nothing will surprise me.
So good to collapse on a bed
in Rome and lie naked,
still wet in the new heat of a day
barely begun and already
too much. But I belong
to it now. I am strange enough,
having put on
the little red shorts and run out into it,
thinking I knew what I was doing.

Six Days with Fra Filippo Lippi's Frescoes in the Duomo at Spoleto

1   *First Day: The Death of Mary*
The mother of God lies wrapped in a burnt-
orange sheet. She is outside, near
pines and moss, as if her bedroom
has become the whole world.
Away from which, at the end,
she turned her exhausted face.
There is something so unposed
about Mary's body, as if death
is a kind of afterthought:
oh, yes, then this happens.
Lippi has trusted us
with so many details, we who
are still alive. It's up to us
to love the world as it really is.

As I leave, a woman stands alone
in the back of the Duomo and prays, touching
her breast and forehead in the ritual way:
here I am again, God, putting the signs
of your suffering on my flesh.
She stares unwaveringly at the altar
and does not turn as I walk past.

2   *Second Day: The Annunciation*
Gabriel cannot look at Mary while he speaks.
Further back from his news
there are six plane trees thick with leaves.
Perhaps after he's gone
she can walk there. Perhaps
those green Umbrian cliffs
will console her for his news:
she must give birth to a child
who will grow, then suffer,
then die. She must become a mother.

3   *Third Day: Mary's Death and the Face of God*
God's memorized all the cues:
it's time to welcome Mary to heaven.
The white beard, the bovine calm.
Perfection seems to make him
sleepy. I keep looking down below
on the painted earth where an astonished
adolescent watches at Mary's bed:
he is pale with grief that she is gone.

Nearby, full-grown saints stand calmly.
They believe all is well. But the pale one
knows. He understands that when the mother goes,
part of life leaves with her,
never to be returned. I envy these saints,
the ones who wear gorgeous blue robes
and walk calmly through the world's
paintings. But it is the boy who guides me,
helps me peer, without turning away,
into the face of Mary's death.

4   *Fourth Day: Lippi in Heaven*
Forget God. Look at the daisies
in heaven. Look at the angel
with the hips. Forget God's droopy-
lidded peace. Don't miss that looped
smile of the angel on the left.

Fra Filippo Lippi,
I read all about you today. They call you
the "dissolute priest": a jealous
husband shot you to death. In *your* heaven,
you just had to paint those robes
that are themselves a kind of flesh,
folds of a second skin
draped teasingly over the first. You must
have loved knowing that centuries later our eyes

would stray from God's dull face
to the hips of angels, their palms, those white
daisy petals so like lily pads slick
with water. All this flesh spread out
across heaven for us to look up to
as we raise our eyes in prayer
and see our world in paradise,
our heaven of cupped hands and earthly needs.

5   *Fifth Day: A Color with which to Drape the Day*
Orange, orange, and again orange. Spread it
over her body, the mother
of God. She's dead now, so give it
some black, some faded blue,
give orange all the room it needs
to drape the world, this lovely tomb.
Break it slowly over the cow
in the manger. Let it stretch out
as skin. The smallest angel
over by the crib: let her be
lightly faded by its smeared
strangeness. And the baby's halo,
a circle of rust or dusty
sunlight, the exact shade that returns
each morning, first thing before
the sun rises, before the birth of God.

6   *Sixth Day: Love, the Manger*
It's not time to plod, to carry,
to pull, to work, to push, to be
milked. It's time to stand still, to adore.
Those animals that have learned to live
from human hands lean forward, their
gray eyes stricken with mild attention.

There's Mary looking down at her child,
there's Joseph looking up toward her.
Meanwhile, the cow concentrates
on the delicious weedy earth and the baby placed on earth.
Love is like this, the amazing
Lippi says: you concentrate and
concentrate, but still there is more to see.

Difficult Mercy

You know how to refuse and you do it well.
This is your most difficult mercy
and it has entered my life through and through.
Whatever comes from me,
you refuse to accept.
Day by day, you are teaching me
how to become worthy of those things
that are not mine to offer:
the sky, these trees, this life
that exists beyond the net of my desire
or pity. Living as I do,
surrounded on all sides
by your refusals, I begin to become worthy.

At Fifty

(A sequence of short prose pieces)

TAGORE: HOMAGES AND VARIATIONS

Inside

Inside the light,
the sky opens and the wind runs wild.

1

It is a Sunday afternoon in Rome and the young policeman is so bored he studies his own fingernails as if they are a profound text with the most serious ramifications. At fifty it makes sense that on your first day in Italy you come here with JoAnn, here where the little café spills out onto the street and the coffee is the best in all Rome, which is to say, in all the world.

It is heaven to arrive in Rome on a Sunday afternoon with a woman who knows how to read maps. The quiet unwinds in the square like a bolt of shimmering cloth and the sunlight is so soft it touches you as a hand would that took all the time in the world to love your flesh.

It makes complete sense that at fifty you get at least one Sunday afternoon in Rome so quiet that the voices of women speaking two streets away carry from stone to stone, like music bouncing off the walls of a cave, that music the Italians call a language. This is the only Sunday afternoon in the world, the first light and the last silence. At fifty, it makes sense that you surround yourself with stone, but warm stone, stone that is like the pulp of a fruit so ripe it has no choice but to fall to earth. You'd better order another coffee; you'd better sit here a long time trying to figure out how to find words for the way the buildings come together in this small square, how they meet at such odd and improbable angles, how they seem to collide, but in the friendliest possible way: like a father wrestling with his children, or a jigsaw puzzle constructed by a child who is putting a city together for the first time, laughing all the while, spending a few centuries at it as you would love to spend a few centuries trying to describe it. Though you'd better stop now, you'd really better lean across the small table covered with green cloth and kiss the woman you love.

Rome / For JoAnn

2

At the Campo dei Fiori, no one seems to mind that you sit on the base of a statue and watch as the vegetables and fruits are unloaded. At fifty, you keep an eye out for others who are also around fifty: the woman in the polka-dot blouse and high heels sorting lettuce; the man setting up shop from his VW bus; the other man in the beard and suspenders who slept all night in front of Pizzeria Virgilio. And straight above, in the slowly whitening sky, a quarter moon, which is also fifty years old. And fifteen or twenty swallows whose age you don't even bother to guess. A white-haired man in shorts sings as he carries a huge silver scale from a small car over to his mound of purple plums. You listen carefully to the ones who reach sixty and can't help singing. The man who slept on the sidewalk pulls a white cap out of his back pocket, puts it on and goes to work picking up trash from the sidewalk and putting it into the nearby bin. At fifty, you could do worse than sit with seven pigeons at dawn near the foot of an ugly statue. You could do worse than walk towards the long strip of sunlight at the far end of the square as two Filipino nuns in dove gray habits move past you, both of them smiling because it's dawn, and it's Rome, and they believe in the dear God of love whose true name is friendship.

Campo dei Fiori / Rome / For Deborah Keenan

3

It is time to lean. And you do just that, your upper back muscles against the cool marble of the Pantheon. Some call it the most perfect building in the world. Why would you ever disagree, the cool marble against your shoulder blades, the whole scooped-out feeling of the place and its comforting circular shape as you lean back and look up at the hole of light far above? There is something ghostly about this space, so gray and calm, so posed: as if it was created in order to bring into being a permanent dusk, a perfectly balanced twilight beyond the reach of time.

You sit down on the marble floor, put your back against the marble wall, and don't move a muscle, here where the shadows come to lay down their burdens of light. It is such a pleasure to turn your back on the city and enter a building composed entirely of marble and soul, a place where no one lives, but anyone who wishes may enter, may stay as long as they want, may lean against marble until its darkness becomes their own, until its circular soul – unlit by anything but a nickel of sky – becomes their soul. You are beginning to learn how to look at light when it enters your life through one small eye so far away, it seems not to be part of your world at all. You may just stay here forever. Here with your marble and your soul, your permanent twilight where once upon a time the gods were worshipped, those dark ones who travel with the speed of whispers, called into being so that the shy, ungainly shapes of our longing might have a home.

Rome

4

Bellini again. A portrait of a man this time, the light on the face
like the light of a summer's afternoon falling across an open field.
A full light, but soft. The man in the painting smiles easily, as if he
is aware that Bellini is filling him with light. It's a small portrait,
set off in a corner. You can stand as close to it as you want. You
are a full twenty years older than the man in the portrait, who
himself has been dead now for over five hundred years. Have you
ever known the utter happiness or untroubled sadness of a face as
Bellini would paint it? You begin to spot such faces here and there –
sometimes in paintings, sometimes on the street. Yesterday at six
in the morning, you were watching the vegetable market being set
up at Campo dei Fiori. A young woman about the age of Bellini's
model in his painting was washing lettuce, then cutting it, using
a knife with a stubby red handle. Her black hair was long and
tangled. She looked half-asleep as she worked, her eyes barely
open. And yet, she worked quickly, her fingers on the lettuce with
the sureness of one who could do what she does in the world for a
living and dream at the same time. Bellini would have painted her
standing at the edge of a little stream: the white of the water in
sunlight; the intense blue of an afternoon sky; the black hair
moving down her back like the fall of water over stone. But mostly
her face. How sleepy, yet how full of life. The eyelids heavy with
tiredness, an excuse for him to give flesh its due. How he loved
the way light turns skin into something you can't wait to touch.
You, too, will spend as much of each day like this as you can,
keeping an eye out for the faces that have taken the day's light
into themselves, then returned it to you as flesh lit from within.

Rome

5

Now it is dawn and the swallows have gone back into their hiding places in the red chimneys across the canal. A wind has arrived, the very smallest wind imaginable, a fluttering on your chest like the breath of a baby asleep in your arms. If your spirit has a home, this is it, here in this city with the dream of water at its heart, and its only purpose to give timelessness a body, a specific shape: Venice.

But this is also the place where you learned that nothing lasts forever. At the heart of timelessness lies contingency. You were here when the news came – suddenly and without warning – that your father was dying. In the kingdom of time, death rules absolutely. For the next month you lived your life under its sway as you sat by the bed of your father.

And then, only last year, JoAnn came down with pneumonia here. She got so sick she would no longer eat, could no longer get out of bed. In the emergency of a dawn that at the time seemed endless, a boat took you both to the airport and an all-day journey that only finished fifteen hours later, in a hospital in your own country.

Two voices from below your hotel window, still sounding sleepy at this early hour, are reflected off stone and water. They seem so close, as if you are in the same room with two people who have known each other a very long time and are lying side by side on the bed behind you, saying their first few words upon waking.

No wonder your soul feels more at home here than in any other place in the world. It was here you learned how to live at the intersection of dreams and mortality. It was here you first learned that there is no protection from death. Places are answers, and Venice is one of those answers for you when the first fishing boats come in from the sea at dawn, after being out all night. You can look down from your window and see Giorgio inspecting the sea bass one by one, rejecting many, letting only those pass into his kitchen that are the right shade of silver, their deaths so fresh that later, as you and JoAnn eat them with parsley and a little oil, you will look across the table at each other, knowing how lucky you are to count yourselves among those who live to die.

Venice

6

You stand in front of an anonymous painting from the Scuola Veneziana. Mary is pensive as she holds her baby, but her face is suffused with something beyond sadness, even beyond love. It is not what she is feeling that matters, but that she has the focus of one who has found her place on earth, and that place is devotion to the truth of who we really are, how we come onto earth thanks to a woman who bears us until we are ready for what we ourselves must bear: that we will love and suffer; that we will die.

The bells ring noon, and the guard sings a chorus of "Bridge over Troubled Water" in English under his breath, an unhurried falsetto with only the slightest accent. No matter how far your life may take you from this moment, you know that Mary will never waver in her devotion, that there is a hard truth at the center of her love, and that no matter what else happens, you, too, have stood before this same truth.

Venice / For Patricia Kirkpatrick

7

You want to understand power. All these years, you've slept at the feet of it like the soldiers in Piero's *Resurrection,* their lovely faces tilted back and filled with that secret intensity we have when we sleep. You look up towards the risen Christ, the one who is awake. It is his face that holds you: not a trace of any emotion, unless wakefulness is itself a kind of feeling. He's who you would be if you were no longer afraid of death. How relaxed he is, knee bent as he props his foot on the top of his tomb as if it were a piece of old furniture. You cannot see as far as he does, with the eyes of one who has died and come back to life. There is nothing he desires other than this: to stand squarely in between the bare trees of winter on his right and the full-leafed trees of summer on his left. To stand quietly at dawn and to proclaim once and for all that the moment of wakefulness – this very moment right now – is the only resurrection anyone will ever need.

Sansepolcro

8

There is no place better to be than the cool darkness of a short summer's night at the goose festival, sitting at a long wooden table under the stars, surrounded on all sides by Italians who understand better than anyone both the art of happiness and the necessity to do it now. While there is time and a reason, goose on the table and wine in the glass.

Spoleto

9

You wake with a feeling of foreboding: something terrible will happen today. And then you remember: it's not what will happen, but what has happened. It was four years ago on this day that your father died. Four years ago that you sat with him, telling him – at long last – that you loved him, though he could no longer hear you.

Here is what you do: you sit at the window at the same time of day that he died and look at the stone wall. It is lined with flower pots, each one filled with geraniums. You sit and you look, and you let the work of beauty enter you, the effort it took to build the stone wall, the care someone puts into seeing that seventeen pots of geraniums thrive. Because that, too, is part of the confusing news that you are meant to receive: not only is there death in the world, but there is beauty. What is confusion anyway, except a mystery for which someone thinks there should be a solution?

On the dusty path outside your window, a small bird about the size of a sparrow. Its small black body is very still in the huge sunlight. There is nowhere else it needs to be other than where it is. You sit at the window and you watch the bird. You have an appointment to keep on the anniversary of your father's death, an appointment with your father, who today has come to you in the body of this small bird, bathing in the soft feathery dust of a hot summer's morning.

Spoleto/In memory of James Wallace Moore

10

It's the father of St. Francis you feel yourself drawn to. Not the saint, but the father of the saint, a man in his fifties, according to Giotto, gray faced and clearly worried. His son, the saint-to-be, has just stripped to show how serious he is about his poverty. A church father has draped a towel around him, but clearly Francis would prefer to be naked. Giotto has painted him with his face turned upwards – and who wouldn't look up if God's hand had just broken through the clouds like a descending airplane? Francis looks absolutely sure of himself in the way that only someone in their early twenties can pull off: his gaze is focused beyond this world. Which means he misses the worry and sadness in his father's face.

You can't possibly argue with what became of this Francis. But how much wiser the father's face is than Francis'; how filled it is with love and suffering. The father is being restrained by a friend. He wants to move into the arms of his son to embrace him, to try to convince him to return home.

But nothing he can say or do will matter in the slightest. Like the father of Francis, you encounter more and more of these moments: what you love you can't control. The one you loved seemed inextricably bound to you, then disappears.

Yes, it is the father you want as your friend. You've got enough of the would-be saint in you already, the perfect young man who thirsts only for more perfection. If you could, you would sit with the father on the day after all this happened. Together you would speak of destroyed hopes, of sons who would be perfect and the pain they must cause. Together you would be amazed at the ways the world has taken each of you by surprise. Maybe you would even shake your heads a little and laugh: "Can you believe he actually took off his clothes?" he might say to you. It seems that you both admire this young man. Who knows, one of you says to the other, what might become of him.

Assisi

11

Go into the kitchen for a fig. Return to the window. Eat the fig slowly. Even the skin of the fig. Eat so slowly you don't miss a thing. Stand near the rain and let your fingers grow sticky with the green and purple juices from a fruit that knows no purpose other than to ripen. When the sun shines, then go out into it. When the rain speaks, then stay at its side and listen well. And when the fig falls, do, by all means, eat it.

Spoleto

12

It's your last full day in Spoleto, in Italy. You spent all of yesterday just looking at Italians being Italians. You watched the old man as he made his way so slowly into the café for his coffee. In one hand was his cane, the other hand firmly on the shoulder of a woman about his age. His left eye was completely gone. Only the socket remained. And his nose, too, was no longer in the shape of a nose; as if, like the eye, it had simply been ripped out of his face. He walked very, very slowly, each step a difficulty that had to be recreated and then solved all over again. But he was still an Italian. He still wanted to be in the world, to go into his bar for a cup of coffee.

This is why you came to Italy: to see this devotion to the world, to the great cup of coffee, to the present understood as a place where it's worth lingering as long as possible, even when the end is near.

It is midnight when you finally walk through the piazza and climb the three flights of stairs to your apartment for the last time. You fall asleep in JoAnn's arms as she reads the paper. "Do you know," she says, "how dangerous it is to pass a truck on the right?"

Spoleto

Your Joy

It was your choice, not mine.
It was you who made me this way,
so that I can never come to the end of myself.
Such is your wish. Your joy
is that I am forever unfinished.
You love how I empty, then fill again
with you. You pocket me
like a flute. Sometimes, at the top of a hill,
you take me out and put me to your lips.
When you breathe into me like that,
I am eternal and new.
At such times, my heart forgets
what a small thing it is. Ages pass
and still you pour me out of your lips.
I have come to love
my own emptiness: without it,
how could I be filled with you?

Jim Moore is the author of *The New Body* (University of Pittsburgh Press, 1975), *What the Bird Sees* (Momentum Press), *How We Missed Belgium* (in collaboration with Deborah Keenan, Milkweed Editions, 1984), and *The Freedom of History* (Milkweed Editions, 1988). In addition, he coedited, with Cary Waterman, the anthology *Minnesota Writes: Poetry* (Milkweed Editions, 1987). His work has been widely published in magazines and anthologies, and he is the recipient of several fellowships and awards for both his prose and his poetry, including grants from the Minnesota State Arts Board, the Bush Foundation, the Jerome Foundation, and a Minnesota Book Award. He has been a teacher of writing for over twenty years. He lives in St. Paul, Minnesota, and is married to photographer JoAnn Verburg.

Designed by Will Powers
Typeset in Sabon
by Stanton Publication Services
Printed on acid-free Booktext Natural paper
by BookCrafters

More Poetry from Milkweed Editions

Amen
Poems by Yehuda Amichai
Translated from the Hebrew
by the author and Ted Hughes

Civil Blood
Jill Breckenridge

Astonishing World
Selected Poems of Ángel González
Translated from the Spanish
by Steven Ford Brown

Mixed Voices
Contemporary Poems about Music
Edited by Emilie Buchwald and Ruth Roston

The Poet Dreaming in the Artist's House
Contemporary Poems about the Visual Arts
Edited by Emilie Buchwald and Ruth Roston

This Sporting Life
Contemporary American Poems
about Sports and Games
Edited by Emilie Buchwald and Ruth Roston

The Color of Mesabi Bones
John Caddy

Mouth to Mouth
Twelve Mexican Women Poets
Edited by Forrest Gander

One Age in a Dream
Diane Glancy

Paul Bunyan's Bearskin
Patricia Goedicke

The Tongues We Speak
Patricia Goedicke

Sacred Hearts
Phebe Hanson

In a Sheep's Eye, Darling
Margaret Hasse

Trusting Your Life to Water and Eternity
Twenty Poems by Olav H. Hauge
Translated from the Norwegian
by Robert Bly

Boxelder Bug Variations
Bill Holm

The Dead Get By with Everything
Bill Holm

Looking for Home
Women Writing about Exile
Edited by Deborah Keenan and Roseann Lloyd

The Freedom of History
Jim Moore

Minnesota Writes Poetry
Edited by Jim Moore and Cary Waterman

The House in the Sand
Prose Poems by Pablo Neruda
Translated from the Spanish
by Dennis Maloney and Clark Zlotchew

Milkweed Editions publishes with the intention of making a humane impact on society, in the belief that literature is a transformative art uniquely able to convey the essential experiences of the human heart and spirit.

To that end, Milkweed Editions publishes distinctive voices of literary merit in handsomely designed, visually dynamic books, exploring the ethical, cultural, and esthetic issues that free societies need continually to address. Milkweed Editions is a not-for-profit press.